~A BINGO BOOK~

Rhode Island Bingo Book

COMPLETE BINGO GAME IN A BOOK

Written By Rebecca Stark

ISBN 978-0-87386-532-6

Educational Books 'n' Bingo

Printed in the U.S.A.

DIRECTIONS

INCLUDED:

List of Terms

Templates for Additional Terms and Clues

2 Clues per Term

30 Unique Bingo Cards

Markers

1. **Either cut apart the book or make copies of ALL the sheets. You might want to make an extra copy of the clue sheets to use for introduction and review. Keep the sheets in an envelope for easy reuse.**

2. Cut apart the call cards with terms and clues.

3. Pass out one bingo card per student. There are enough for a class of 30.

4. Pass out markers. You may cut apart the markers included in this book or use any other small items of your choice.

5. Decide whether or not you will require the entire card to be filled. Requiring the entire card to be filled provides a better review. However, if you have a short time to fill, you may prefer to have them do the just the border or some other format. Tell the class before you begin what is required.

6. There are 50 terms. Read the list before you begin. If there are any terms that have not been covered in class, you may want to read to the students the term and clues before you begin.

7. There is a blank space in the middle of each card. You can instruct the students to use it as a free space or you can write in answers to cover terms not included. Of course, in this case you would create your own clues. (Templates provided.)

8. Shuffle the cards and place them in a pile. Two or three clues are provided for each term. If you plan to play the game with the same group more than once, you might want to choose a different clue for each game. If not, you may choose to use more than one clue.

9. Be sure to keep the cards you have used for the present game in a separate pile. When a student calls, "Bingo," he or she will have to verify that the correct answers are on his or her card AND that the markers were placed in response to the proper questions. Pull out the cards that are on the student's card keeping them in the order they were used in the game. Read each clue as it was given and ask the student to identify the correct answer from his or her card.

10. If the student has the correct answers on the card AND has shown that they were marked in response to the *correct questions,* then that student is the winner and the game is over. If the student does not have the correct answers on the card OR he or she marked the answers in response to *the wrong questions,* then the game continues until there is a proper winner.

11. If you want to play again, reshuffle the cards and begin again.

Have fun!

TERMS INCLUDED

Agricultural

Atlantic Ocean

Apple(s)

Battle of Rhode Island

Block Island

Border (-ed)

Bowenite

Breakers

Moses Brown

Ambrose Burnside

Civil War

Climate

Coastal Lowlands

Coffee Milk

George M. Cohan

County (-ies)

Cranston

Cumberlandite

Eastern New England Upland

Executive Branch

Flag

Crescent Park Carousel

Nathanael Greene

Hope

Anne Hutchinson

Industrial Revolution

Industries

Jerimoth Hill

Judicial Branch

King Philip

Legislative Branch

Narragansett Bay

Native American

New England

Newport

Ocean State

Pell Bridge

Oliver Hazard Perry

Portsmouth

Providence

Quahaug

Red Maple

Rhode Island Red

River(s)

Scituate Reservoir

Samuel Slater

Song(s)

Union

Warwick

Roger Williams

Rhode Island Bingo

Additional Terms

Choose as many additional terms as you would like and write them in the squares. Repeat each as desired.
Cut out the squares and randomly distribute them to the class.
Instruct the students to place their square on the center space of their card.

Rhode Island Bingo

Clues for Additional Terms

Write three clues for each of your additional terms.

_____ 1. 2. 3.	_____ 1. 2. 3.
_____ 1. 2. 3.	_____ 1. 2. 3.
_____ 1. 2. 3.	_____ 1. 2. 3.

Rhode Island Bingo

Agricultural 1. The most important ___ products are greenhouse and nursery products, sweet corn, dairy products, potatoes, and cattle and calves. 2. Dairy products account for about 5% of Rhode Island's total receipts from ___ products.	**Atlantic Ocean** 1. Rhode Island is bordered on the east by the ___. 2. Rhode Island has over 400 miles of coastline. This includes Narragansett Bay, which extends inland from the ___ and extends north to the center of the state.
Apple(s) 1. The Rhode Island greening ___ is the official state fruit. 2. Rhode Island greening ___ are crisp; they keep their sharp taste in cooking.	**Battle of Rhode Island** 1. The ___ was fought on August 29, 1778. John Sullivan, Nathanael Greene, and Marquis de Lafayette were officerss on the American side. 2. Major General Sir Robert Pigot was the British leader at this Revolutionary War battle.
Block Island 1. ___ is about 12 miles south of the mainland. It is known for its rugged coastal bluffs. 2. ___ is named for the Dutch trader and navigator who explored the area and named this island.	**Border (-ed)** 1. Massachusetts and Connecticut ___ Rhode Island. 2. Rhode Island is ___ on the east by the Atlantic Ocean.
Bowenite 1. ___ is the state mineral. 2. This semi-precious green gemstone is a close relative of jade.	**Breakers** 1. The ___ was the summer home of Cornelius Vanderbilt II. 2. This mansion was built in 1895. It is the most-visited attraction in Rhode Island.
Moses Brown 1. ___ was a co-founder of Brown University. 2. ___ was an abolitionist and industrialist. He funded some of the first textile mills during the American Industrial Revolution, including Slater Mill. Rhode Island Bingo	**Ambrose Burnside** 1. ___ was a soldier, railroad executive, inventor, industrialist, and politician. 2. This general of the Union Army later became the 30th governor of Rhode Island. © Barbara M. Peller

Civil War 1. Like all of New England, Rhode Island remained loyal to the Union during the ___. 2. Like the other northern states, Rhode Island's industries supplied the Union Army with the materials it needed to win the ___.	**Climate** 1. Rhode Island has a humid continental ___, with cold winters and short summers. 2. Rhode Island's ___ is characterized by large seasonal temperature differences: cold winters and warm to hot—and often humid—summers.
Coastal Lowlands 1. The ___ cover about two-thirds of the state. The region extends to the islands in the Narragansett Bay. 2. Sandy beaches and plains are along the coast in this geographic region. Farther inland are low hills and grassy slopes.	**Coffee Milk** 1. ___ is the state drink. 2. This flavored milk is made with coffee syrup.
George M. Cohan 1. ___ was born on July 3, 1878, in Providence. 2. In 1936, ___ received a Congressional Gold Medal in recognition for his patriotic songs "Over There" and "A Grand Old Flag."	**County (-ies)** 1. There are 5 ___ in Rhode Island. 2. Although Rhode Island is divided into 5 ___, there is no ___ government.
Cranston 1. The city of ___ was once known as Pawtuxet. 2. ___ was created in 1754 from a portion of Providence north of the Pawtuxet River. It is part of the Providence metropolitan area.	**Cumberlandite** 1. This heavy black or dark brown rock with white markings is the state rock. 2. Due to its high amounts of iron, ___ is slightly magnetic.
Eastern New England Upland 1. The ___ covers the northwestern third of Rhode Island. 2. The ___ is characterized by rolling hills with lakes and ponds scattered among the hills. The highest natural point in the state, Jerimoth Hill, is in this region.	**Executive Branch** 1. The governor and various agencies comprise the ___ of government. 2. The governor is the head of the ___. The present-day governor is [fill in].

Rhode Island Bingo

© Barbara M. Peller

Flag 1. The state ___ has a white field and is fringed in gold. In the center is a gold anchor surrounded by thirteen golden stars. 2. A blue ribbon with the state motto in gold letters is beneath the anchor on the state ___.	**Crescent Park Carousel** 1. The ___ was part of a Victorian-era amusement park. It was designed and built in 1895 by Charles I.D. Looff, a native of Denmark. 2. The ___ is the official state symbol of American folk art. It is also a National Historic Landmark.
Nathanael Greene 1. When news of the battle of Bunker Hill spread, Rhode Island raised three regiments of troops and placed ___ at their head as general. 2. General Washington appointed ___ quartermaster-general with the responsibility of getting food for the troops at Valley Forge.	**Hope** 1. ___ is the state motto. 2. The state motto, ___, is on both the state flag and the state seal.
Anne Hutchinson 1. ___ was banished from Massachusetts Bay for expressing religious beliefs that were different from those of the colony's rulers. 2. With encouragement from Roger Williams, ___ and her supporters established the settlement of Portsmouth in Providence Plantation.	**Industrial Revolution** 1. Many immigrants arrived in Rhode Island in the 1800s because the ___ took hold there quickly. 2. Towns in Rhode Island grew in the 1800s because of the ___.
Industries 1. Electrical equipment, jewelry, and computer and electronics products are important ___. 2. Tourism and fishing are also important ___.	**Jerimoth Hill** 1. At 812 feet, ___ is the highest natural point in the state. 2. ___ is in the town of Foster, near the Connecticut border. It is in the Eastern New England Upland Region.
Judicial Branch 1. The ___ of the state government interprets Rhode Island laws. There are six state court systems. 2. The Supreme Court is the highest court of the ___. It hears all appeals and has the final interpretation of the law.	**King Philip** 1. ___'s real name was Metacomet. He was the chief of the Wampanoag Indians. 2. ___'s War of 1675–1678 was a conflict between Native Americans and English colonists and their Native American allies.

Rhode Island Bingo

Legislative Branch	**Narragansett Bay**
1. The ___ of government, called the General Assembly, comprises the Senate and the House of Representatives. 2. The ___ makes the laws.	1. Narragansett Bay is a northern extension of the Atlantic Ocean. It contains three major islands: Aquidneck, Conanicut, and Prudence. 2. The largest island in ___ is Aquidneck. Newport is on this island.
Native American	**New England**
1. When the Europeans arrived, ___ tribes, including the Wampanoag, Narragansett, and Niantic, occupied most of the area now known as Rhode Island. 2. Today there is one federally recognized ___ tribe: the Narragansett Indian Tribe. Their reservation is in Bristol.	1. ___ comprises Maine, New Hampshire, Vermont, Massachusetts, Rhode Island, and Connecticut. 2. The ___ Colonies of British America included the Massachusetts Bay Colony, Connecticut Colony, Colony of Rhode Island and Providence Plantations, and Province of New Hampshire.
Newport	**Ocean State**
1. ___ is a popular tourist spot because of the mansions of the Gilded Age. The Breakers, Chateau-sur-Mer, The Elms, Marble House, and Rosecliff are a few of those mansions. 2. The Vanderbilts and Astors were among those families with mansions in ___. They referred to them as their summer "cottages."	1. Rhode Island is called the ___. 2. Rhode Island gets this nickname because of its 400 miles of shoreline. All Rhode Islanders live within a 30-minute drive to the Atlantic Ocean or Narragansett Bay.
Pell Bridge	**Oliver Hazard Perry**
1. This suspension bridge is commonly known as the Newport Bridge. 2. ___ connects Newport on Aquidneck Island and Jamestown on Conanicut Island. Conanicut Island is connected to the mainland by the Jamestown Verrazzano Bridge.	1. This naval officer was the hero of the Battle of Lake Erie during the War of 1812. He received a Congressional Gold Medal. 2. The *SSV* ___ is the state educational sailing vessel; it is named for a naval hero of the War of 1812.
Portsmouth	**Providence**
1. ___ was settled in 1638 by a group of religious dissenters from Boston Colony. 2. Anne Hutchinson, Dr. John Clarke, and William Coddington were the founders of ___.	1. ___ is the capital and most populous city in Rhode Island. 2. ___ was one of the first cities in the country to industrialize. It became noted for its jewelry and silverware industry.

Rhode Island Bingo

Quahaug 1. The ___ is the state shell. 2. Native Americans used the ___ shells to make wampum beads. Beads that were made from the purple part of the shell were the most valuable form of wampum.	**Red Maple** 1. ___ is the state tree. 2. The ___ provides beautiful fall foliage. Its leaves turn gold, purple, and scarlet.
Rhode Island Red 1. The ___ is the state bird. 2. The___ is raised for meat and eggs. It is also a show bird.	**River(s)** 1. Major ___ include the Blackstone, Pawcatuck, Pawtuxet, and Wood. 2. Although called a ___, the Sakonnet is actually a saltwater strait. It separates Aquidneck Island from the eastern portion of Newport County.
Scituate Reservoir 1. ___ Reservoir is the largest inland body of water in the state. 2. The original spelling of this town's name was "Satuit," a native Indian word meaning "cold brook" or "cold river." The town was a part of Providence until 1731.	**Samuel Slater** 1. ___ founded the first textile mill in the United States in Pawtucket, Rhode Island. 2. ___ is known as the "Father of the American Textile Industry" and the "Father of the American Industrial Revolution."
Song(s) 1. "Rhode Island, It's For Me" is the official state ___. 2. In addition to an official state ___, there is a state march. "Rhode Island" is the state march.	**Union** 1. Rhode Island entered the ___ on May 29, 1790. It was the last of the original 13 states to ratify the Constitution. 2. Rhode Island is the smallest state in the ___, but it is densely populated.
Warwick 1. ___ is the second largest city in the state. 2. ___ was the site of what became known as the Gaspée Affair. Local patriots boarded the *HMS Gaspée* and burned it in reaction to the Stamp Act. Rhode Island Bingo	**Roger Williams** 1. After being banished from the Massachusetts Bay Colony for his religious views, ___ founded Providence Plantation. 2. ___ founded Providence Plantation at the tip of Narragansett Bay on land granted to him by the Narragansett tribe.

Rhode Island Bingo

Oliver Hazard Perry	Agricultural	Apple(s)	Eastern New England Upland	Block Island
Cranston	Atlantic Ocean	Union	King Philip	Quahaug
Song(s)	Judicial Branch		Newport	Warwick
Samuel Slater	Providence	Scituate Reservoir	Jerimoth Hill	Narragansett Bay
New England	Crescent Park Carousel	Coffee Milk	Rhode Island Red	Anne Hutchinson

Rhode Island Bingo: Card No. 1

Rhode Island Bingo

Samuel Slater	Song(s)	Hope	Portsmouth	Industries
Narragansett Bay	George M. Cohan	Breakers	Providence	Native American
Ambrose Burnside	Crescent Park Carousel		Nathanael Greene	Scituate Reservoir
Ocean State	Pell Bridge	Judicial Branch	Roger Williams	Block Island
Quahaug	Union	Coffee Milk	Cranston	Rhode Island Red

Rhode Island Bingo

Crescent Park Carousel	Scituate Reservoir	George M. Cohan	Jerimoth Hill	Song(s)
Narragansett Bay	Atlantic Ocean	Moses Brown	Agricultural	Flag
Providence	Union		Native American	Battle of Rhode Island
Judicial Branch	Ambrose Burnside	New England	Ocean State	Hope
Rhode Island Red	Civil War	Coffee Milk	Roger Williams	Industries

Rhode Island Bingo: Card No. 3

Rhode Island Bingo

Judicial Branch	Native American	Apple(s)	Civil War	Industries
Legislative Branch	Bowenite	Agricultural	Portsmouth	Song(s)
Newport	Ocean State		Anne Hutchinson	Eastern New England Upland
Scituate Reservoir	Atlantic Ocean	Union	Coffee Milk	Breakers
Climate	Quahaug	Border (-ed)	Rhode Island Red	Warwick

Rhode Island Bingo

Quahaug	Block Island	Providence	Breakers	Civil War
Legislative Branch	Scituate Reservoir	Moses Brown	Nathanael Greene	Atlantic Ocean
Apple(s)	Warwick		King Philip	Executive Branch
Anne Hutchinson	Industries	Oliver Hazard Perry	Roger Williams	Coastal Lowlands
George M. Cohan	Coffee Milk	Song(s)	Judicial Branch	Newport

Rhode Island Bingo: Card No. 5

Rhode Island Bingo

Battle of Rhode Island	Native American	Hope	Industries	Warwick
Jerimoth Hill	Providence	Coastal Lowlands	Agricultural	Song(s)
Portsmouth	Climate		Bowenite	Nathanael Greene
Coffee Milk	New England	Roger Williams	Border (-ed)	Apple(s)
Narragansett Bay	Breakers	Oliver Hazard Perry	Newport	County (-ies)

Rhode Island Bingo

Oliver Hazard Perry	Native American	Executive Branch	Scituate Reservoir	George M. Cohan
Narragansett Bay	Industries	Crescent Park Carousel	Atlantic Ocean	Legislative Branch
Warwick	Eastern New England Upland		Nathanael Greene	Bowenite
Judicial Branch	Ocean State	Moses Brown	Samuel Slater	Ambrose Burnside
Coffee Milk	Civil War	Roger Williams	Border (-ed)	Battle of Rhode Island

Rhode Island Bingo: Card No. 7

Rhode Island Bingo

Newport	Native American	Cumberlandite	Jerimoth Hill	Bowenite
Legislative Branch	Apple(s)	Portsmouth	Warwick	Breakers
County (-ies)	Civil War		Industries	Block Island
Rhode Island Red	Judicial Branch	Samuel Slater	Climate	Ocean State
Union	Coffee Milk	Border (-ed)	Providence	Narragansett Bay

Rhode Island Bingo

Nathanael Greene	George M. Cohan	Crescent Park Carousel	County (-ies)	Civil War
Climate	Industries	Newport	Providence	Native American
Flag	Oliver Hazard Perry		Atlantic Ocean	Cumberlandite
Coastal Lowlands	Block Island	New England	King Philip	Executive Branch
Ocean State	Roger Williams	Moses Brown	Samuel Slater	Anne Hutchinson

Rhode Island Bingo

Samuel Slater	Jerimoth Hill	Bowenite	Portsmouth	County (-ies)
Warwick	Breakers	Agricultural	Atlantic Ocean	Industries
Civil War	Native American		Eastern New England Upland	Ambrose Burnside
New England	Anne Hutchinson	Coastal Lowlands	Roger Williams	Flag
Moses Brown	Narragansett Bay	Hope	Quahaug	Newport

Rhode Island Bingo

Battle of Rhode Island	Native American	Providence	Coastal Lowlands	Narragansett Bay
Cumberlandite	Flag	King Philip	Nathanael Greene	Agricultural
Legislative Branch	Industries		Hope	Crescent Park Carousel
Moses Brown	Song(s)	Roger Williams	Civil War	Samuel Slater
Climate	Coffee Milk	Oliver Hazard Perry	Border (-ed)	George M. Cohan

Rhode Island Bingo

George M. Cohan	Block Island	Flag	Jerimoth Hill	Nathanael Greene
Crescent Park Carousel	Narragansett Bay	Apple(s)	Border (-ed)	Atlantic Ocean
Oliver Hazard Perry	Executive Branch		Warwick	Portsmouth
Coffee Milk	Ocean State	Industries	Samuel Slater	Legislative Branch
Native American	Cumberlandite	Civil War	Climate	Breakers

Rhode Island Bingo: Card No. 12

Rhode Island Bingo

Coastal Lowlands	Block Island	Battle of Rhode Island	Flag	Warwick
Apple(s)	Cumberlandite	Industries	Nathanael Greene	Ambrose Burnside
Jerimoth Hill	Breakers		Crescent Park Carousel	Executive Branch
Newport	Roger Williams	Bowenite	Civil War	Samuel Slater
Coffee Milk	Anne Hutchinson	Border (-ed)	Oliver Hazard Perry	King Philip

Rhode Island Bingo: Card No. 13

Rhode Island
Bingo

Warwick	Har	Battle of Rhode Island	Block Island	Coastal Wetlands
Amtrak Carriers			Combahee	
				Mammoth
King Philip				Coffee Milk

Rhode Island Bingo

Cranston	Industries	Providence	Nathanael Greene	Climate
Breakers	Oliver Hazard Perry	Flag	Atlantic Ocean	Native American
Coastal Lowlands	Eastern New England Upland		Hope	Moses Brown
Anne Hutchinson	Roger Williams	Civil War	Bowenite	Battle of Rhode Island
Coffee Milk	Portsmouth	Ambrose Burnside	Narragansett Bay	Newport

Rhode Island Bingo

King Philip	Nathanael Greene	Providence	George M. Cohan	Jerimoth Hill
Battle of Rhode Island	Hope	Agricultural	Apple(s)	Climate
Warwick	Oliver Hazard Perry		Song(s)	Native American
Coffee Milk	Flag	Cumberlandite	Roger Williams	Coastal Lowlands
Narragansett Bay	Ocean State	Border (-ed)	County (-ies)	Crescent Park Carousel

Rhode Island Bingo: Card No. 15

Rhode Island Bingo

Bowenite	Flag	Cumberlandite	County (-ies)	Pell Bridge
Portsmouth	Ambrose Burnside	Executive Branch	Legislative Branch	Eastern New England Upland
Coastal Lowlands	Block Island		Warwick	Crescent Park Carousel
Judicial Branch	Breakers	Coffee Milk	King Philip	Samuel Slater
Climate	River(s)	Border (-ed)	Ocean State	Native American

Rhode Island Bingo: Card No. 16

© Barbara M. Peller

Rhode Island Bingo

Moses Brown	Red Maple	Industrial Revolution	Flag	Cranston
King Philip	Climate	Roger Williams	Eastern New England Upland	Executive Branch
Nathanael Greene	Newport		River(s)	Cumberlandite
Anne Hutchinson	Narragansett Bay	Samuel Slater	Providence	Ambrose Burnside
New England	Coastal Lowlands	George M. Cohan	Jerimoth Hill	Block Island

Rhode Island Bingo

County (-ies)	Civil War	Breakers	Coastal Lowlands	Portsmouth
Native American	Moses Brown	New England	Warwick	Climate
Nathanael Greene	Ambrose Burnside		Industrial Revolution	Apple(s)
Block Island	Agricultural	Roger Williams	Samuel Slater	Hope
River(s)	Flag	Providence	Red Maple	Battle of Rhode Island

Rhode Island Bingo

Warwick	Battle of Rhode Island	Flag	Cumberlandite	Samuel Slater
King Philip	Jerimoth Hill	Native American	George M. Cohan	Eastern New England Upland
Red Maple	Civil War		Atlantic Ocean	Song(s)
Hope	River(s)	New England	Ocean State	Industrial Revolution
Apple(s)	Pell Bridge	Narragansett Bay	Newport	Border (-ed)

Rhode Island Bingo

Cranston	Red Maple	Jerimoth Hill	Flag	Border (-ed)
Breakers	Crescent Park Carousel	Legislative Branch	New England	Portsmouth
Block Island	Executive Branch		Judicial Branch	Agricultural
Quahaug	Union	Rhode Island Red	Ocean State	River(s)
Scituate Reservoir	Newport	Pell Bridge	Samuel Slater	Industrial Revolution

Rhode Island Bingo: Card No. 20

© Barbara M. Peller

Rhode Island Bingo

King Philip	Battle of Rhode Island	Legislative Branch	Flag	Quahaug
Block Island	Industrial Revolution	Bowenite	Cumberlandite	Oliver Hazard Perry
Ambrose Burnside	Narragansett Bay		Red Maple	Providence
New England	George M. Cohan	River(s)	Anne Hutchinson	Newport
Judicial Branch	Pell Bridge	Border (-ed)	Moses Brown	Ocean State

Rhode Island Bingo: Card No. 21

Rhode Island Bingo

County (-ies)	Hope	Industrial Revolution	Apple(s)	Coastal Lowlands
Portsmouth	Jerimoth Hill	Song(s)	Cumberlandite	Atlantic Ocean
Breakers	Eastern New England Upland		Oliver Hazard Perry	Executive Branch
River(s)	Anne Hutchinson	Ocean State	Agricultural	Legislative Branch
Pell Bridge	Moses Brown	Red Maple	Ambrose Burnside	Judicial Branch

Rhode Island Bingo: Card No. 22

Rhode Island Bingo

Bowenite	Red Maple	George M. Cohan	Apple(s)	Border (-ed)
Battle of Rhode Island	Cranston	Narragansett Bay	King Philip	Agricultural
Hope	Coastal Lowlands		Rhode Island Red	Oliver Hazard Perry
Ambrose Burnside	Pell Bridge	River(s)	Moses Brown	Ocean State
Quahaug	Union	Newport	New England	Industrial Revolution

Rhode Island Bingo

Bowenite	Newport	Cranston	Red Maple	Cumberlandite
Industrial Revolution	Border (-ed)	Legislative Branch	Portsmouth	Oliver Hazard Perry
Executive Branch	County (-ies)		Coastal Lowlands	Ambrose Burnside
Quahaug	Rhode Island Red	River(s)	Moses Brown	Block Island
Scituate Reservoir	Judicial Branch	Pell Bridge	Jerimoth Hill	Union

Rhode Island Bingo

Judicial Branch	Legislative Branch	Red Maple	Providence	Industrial Revolution
Agricultural	Block Island	King Philip	Bowenite	Atlantic Ocean
Anne Hutchinson	Cumberlandite		Rhode Island Red	River(s)
Song(s)	Quahaug	Union	Pell Bridge	Eastern New England Upland
Border (-ed)	Cranston	Breakers	Climate	Scituate Reservoir

Rhode Island Bingo

Industrial Revolution	Red Maple	Hope	Portsmouth	County (-ies)
New England	Jerimoth Hill	Cumberlandite	Cranston	Bowenite
Anne Hutchinson	Rhode Island Red		Eastern New England Upland	Judicial Branch
Moses Brown	Apple(s)	Quahaug	Pell Bridge	River(s)
Executive Branch	Climate	Providence	Union	Scituate Reservoir

Rhode Island Bingo

Hope	Breakers	Red Maple	Cranston	Crescent Park Carousel
Quahaug	Rhode Island Red	King Philip	River(s)	Atlantic Ocean
Roger Williams	Union		Pell Bridge	Judicial Branch
County (-ies)	Battle of Rhode Island	Legislative Branch	Scituate Reservoir	Agricultural
Climate	Eastern New England Upland	Industrial Revolution	Song(s)	Executive Branch

Rhode Island Bingo: Card No. 27

Rhode Island
Bingo

Rhode Island Bingo

Hope	Cranston	Song(s)	Red Maple	Bowenite
Crescent Park Carousel	Industrial Revolution	Rhode Island Red	Portsmouth	Eastern New England Upland
Union	Ambrose Burnside		Executive Branch	New England
Samuel Slater	County (-ies)	Narragansett Bay	Pell Bridge	River(s)
Apple(s)	Nathanael Greene	Climate	Scituate Reservoir	Quahaug

© Barbara M. Peller

Rhode Island Bingo

Industrial Revolution	Cranston	County (-ies)	King Philip	Nathanael Greene
Ocean State	New England	Legislative Branch	Executive Branch	Song(s)
Anne Hutchinson	Rhode Island Red		Atlantic Ocean	Red Maple
Crescent Park Carousel	Quahaug	Industries	Pell Bridge	River(s)
Bowenite	Cumberlandite	Scituate Reservoir	Battle of Rhode Island	Union

Rhode Island Bingo: Card No. 29

Rhode Island Bingo

Civil War	Red Maple	Portsmouth	Nathanael Greene	River(s)
Agricultural	Cranston	Hope	Eastern New England Upland	Atlantic Ocean
Anne Hutchinson	Coastal Lowlands		Executive Branch	Legislative Branch
Scituate Reservoir	Battle of Rhode Island	Apple(s)	Pell Bridge	Rhode Island Red
Quahaug	Warwick	Union	Industrial Revolution	Song(s)